I0189906

# *The* ValueGiver

# Study Guide

## DALLAS ELDER

*The ValueGiver Study Guide*
*By Dallas Elder*
Copyright © 2013 by Dallas Elder
All Rights Reserved
**ISBN-13: 978-0615756585**
**ISBN-10: 0615756581**

Published by Grace Covenant

This book and the parts thereof may not be reproduced in any form, stored in a retrieval system or transmitted in any form by any means (electronic, mechanical, photocopy, recording or otherwise) without prior written permission of the author, except as provided by United States of America copyright law.

All Scripture quotations, unless otherwise indicated, are taken from the *Holy Bible, New International Version*®. NIV®. Copyright © 1973, 1978, 1984 by Biblica, Inc.™ Used by permission of Zondervan. All rights reserved worldwide. www.zondervan.com.

Scripture quotations marked NLT are taken from the *Holy Bible*, New Living Translation, copyright © 1996, 2004, 2007 by Tyndale House Foundation. Used by permission of Tyndale House Publishers, Inc., Carol Stream, Illinois 60188. All rights reserved.

Revised Standard Version of the Bible, copyright 1952 [2nd edition, 1971] by the Division of Christian Education of the National Council of the Churches of Christ in the United States of America. Used by permission. All rights reserved.

Scripture taken from *The Message*. Copyright © 1993, 1994, 1995, 1996, 2000, 2001, 2002. Used by permission of NavPress Publishing Group.

Quotations taken from *The ValueGiver* by Dallas Elder. Copyright © 2011 by Dallas Elder. Published by Advantage Books, Longwood, FL.

# Table of Contents

# Study Guide

## for

# The ValueGiver

## Going Deeper

This study guide is intended to help people to further explore and examine the life changing truths found in *The ValueGiver*. It is a companion resource for individuals and useful in small groups, to deepen discovery and discussion of the topics mentioned in the book. Receiving and realizing our true worth as a person created with divine intention is revolutionizing and transforming. It enables us to embrace our significance, live with confidence, pursue our purpose and realize our destiny. As we receive our true value through the redeeming grace and power of God, we are empowered to live up to our personal potential and we become a value-giving agent to redeem and empower others. Our transformation leads to the transformation of others, and we bring significant change to our world. We contribute to making our world an *appreciating* (increasing-value) environment rather than a *depreciating* (decreasing-value) one. We live out of our truly valued self and assign true worth to others. God helps us to overcome the devaluing experiences of life. We discover the depth with which we are loved and cherished by The ValueGiver. In turn, we learn to respect, honor and assign true worth to others. We become ValueGivers.

# SESSION 1...*Introduction*

# Understanding Our World

*Read Introduction of *The ValueGiver.*

**Abraham Lincoln said, "I can see how man could look upon the world and be an atheist, but I cannot conceive how he could look into the heavens and say there is no God."**

### Our Confusing World

The world can be a confusing place. It has landscapes of stunning beauty, inspiring vistas and awesome expanses. Its mass and variety reveals the supreme power of its Maker. Its intricate detail and sequential interaction underscores the supernatural genius of the Creator. There is bliss in its beauty and the message that it was crafted with great care for its inhabitants. On the other hand there appears to be a randomness and harshness to life on this rock. There are natural disasters, tragic events, evil crusades, heinous crimes, abuses and injustices. For the average person, the dichotomy stimulates a number of questions. There is beauty and there is brokenness.

## Discovery Questions

1. What are some of the attributes you know about God?

   _____    _____

   _____    _____

   _____    _____

   _____    _____

2. As you look at the world around you, what are some of the harsh realities you see?

   _____    _____

   _____    _____

   _____    _____

   _____    _____

3.  Based on what you know of God and what you see in the world, what is one question you would like to ask God?

_____

_____


**Scripture Reference:** Romans 8:20–22

*For the creation was subjected to frustration, not by its own choice, but by the will of the one who subjected it, in hope that the creation itself will be liberated from its bondage to decay and brought into the glorious freedom of the children of God. We know that the whole creation has been groaning as in the pains of child birth right up to the present time.*

### Our Damaged World

When God created the world, He created it as a perfect, peaceful paradise. Everything was in right relationship. All of creation worked in absolute harmony. It was a serene, secure and sacred home that God designed and constructed for mankind. God created man with the freedom to make choices. He counseled man on what was right but gave mankind the liberty to choose from life options. When mankind sinned, it opened the door for evil to infiltrate creation. This is often called "the fall of man." Man was created to live in right relationship and harmony with God and creation. God's original design for the world became damaged through man's wrongful and sinful choices. The world was no longer a harmonious place but was askew and predominantly tilted toward disharmony. The divine design became damaged, disharmonious and destructive. This is why the world (creation) groans.

### Discovery Question

4.  What would you see as damages to our world, evil effects ushered in by the fall of man? How has God's original design been damaged?

_____

_____

_____

_____


### Our Depreciating World

Because our world is a damaged and disharmonious place to live, it becomes a depreciating environment. Its evil undercurrents cut away at the worth and personhood of individuals. It is a depreciating onslaught of events, experiences and value statements aimed at diminishing a person's dignity and destiny. It is an attempt to chain people in bondage to the broken design where cruelty and destruction reigns and all hope for a better future is lost. Through the unpleasant and hurtful experiences of rejections, abuse, injustice, prejudice and our own bad judgments, image labels are fabricated and fixed to our being. They become marks and scars that we bear, shaping us as damaged goods and destined to live life as such. We think of ourselves as broken, with limited potential. Our life vision is impaired by the way we view our self. The depreciating world bombards our soul with life-robbing statements derived from our painful experiences, cruel criticisms of the self-absorbed and the inaccurate conclusions of self-centered social structures. The spirits of evil at work in our world spin these diabolical statements toward us, to assess us with diminished value and to attach them to us as a summation of our net worth. They distort our true created image and distance us from God's divine intention. They rob us of our value, our significance, our purpose and our destiny. This is our "groan," and we join the chorus with the rest of creation.

**Discovery Question**

5. What are examples of depreciating statements that devalue people?

_____

_____

_____

_____

**Scripture Reference:** Revelation 21:5

*He who was seated on the throne said, "I am making everything new!" Then he said, "Write this down, for these words are trustworthy and true."*

## Redeeming Our World

God reigns upon His throne and over His creation. While the world reflects the damage, the depreciation and the destructive powers initiated by the sinfulness of man, God is at work to redeem and restore mankind and all creation. The reason He sent Jesus into the world was to restore creation back to its original design. Man can be forgiven and redeemed through faith in Jesus Christ. Through a relationship with God, we become a new creation. This is God's redeeming plan to make new all of creation by removing the damage and healing its brokenness. He begins with making the people of the world who believe in Him, new creations. He will finish His redemptive project with the forming of a new heaven and a new earth. He will make "everything new."

*But God demonstrates his own love for us in this: While we were still sinners, Christ died for us. Romans 5:8*

The redeeming work of God in people provides for the forgiveness of their sins, the restoration of right relationship to Him, the deposit of His Spirit to live in them and the gift of eternal life in Heaven. And much more. The redeeming work of God can bring healing to the damages we have received through our life in the depreciating world. Jesus is the Appreciator. He redeems us for our true value. He touches hurts that have poisoned our thinking and positioned us for less than our potential. He removes disgrace and restores dignity. He replaces the destructive image messages with affirming truths about our identity in Him. He lifts our eyes to see life from Heaven's side of things and to embrace God's vision and divine intention for us. He convinces us that God truly loves us. He encourages us to trust Him and allow Him to help us become a new creation. Through His grace and power, He redeems us and positions us to become a person of value, significance, purpose and destiny. He is The ValueGiver.

No person is without worth. No person is beyond redemption–if they want to be redeemed. No amount of harsh life circumstances, poor choices, self-effacement, personal rejection, shameful deeds or the merciless negative assessment of others, can lower your value in the sight of God. He still considers you worth redeeming, worth loving, worth embracing, worth blessing. He affirms you toward your divine destiny which He has uniquely crafted for you. Dallas Elder *The ValueGiver p.13*

**Summary Response**

⇒ What is one observation, insight or conclusion that you can draw from this lesson?

_____

_____

_____

_____

---

**WORTH CONSIDERATION**

Our world is a depreciating place with a rampant current of devaluing messages and life experiences. Evil forces press these into our souls in an attempt to distort God's divine design of value, significance and purpose. We get caught in the evil swirl of the world and perpetuate its diminishing effects on others. When we receive our true value through truth, grace and faith in Jesus Christ, The ValueGiver, we come to own God's original design and divine intention for us. We understand our true worth. As valued persons, we become a rising tide of appreciation that increases value in others and lifts them to new levels of life.

# SESSION 2...*Chapter 1*

# The Lost and the Least

*Read chapter 1 of *The ValueGiver*.

**When we recall the presence of Jesus amid his contemporaries, we remember that it was especially those who were considered marginal, disreputable, and truly needy that were welcomed by Jesus. Those who sought to protect Jesus from being contaminated or "violated" by association with sinners were themselves scolded by him.[1] Ray Anderson**

### Life's Broken Road

Sometimes the way life has unfolded for us is not what we had envisioned as we started out. We had ambitions, aspirations, inspirations and dreams to be fulfilled. However, things didn't work out as we had planned. There were unexpected events, disappointments, and possibly, we made unwise choices along the way. These twists and turns of life led us off course and we are left with some unfulfilled expectations and broken dreams. Daily, we live with the lament and, sometimes, shame of those losses. Unfortunately, our life can get buried under the debris of these misadventures and misfortunes. The more time passes, the deeper the despair and the more hopeless we feel. We had our shot at life and we misfired. We live with the pain of poor choices and the shame it left on our lives. We drag them along with us as our legacy. We lived and loved and lost. We find it difficult to enjoy the present, believe for a better future because of the disappointments of our past.

**Scripture Reference:** Read Luke 7:36–50

**Discovery Questions**

1. Why do you think the woman was drawn to Jesus?

_____

_____

_____

2. What do you think is the significance of the woman pouring out her tears on the feet of Jesus?

_____

_____

_____

## Offering of Tears

There was a tradition and understanding for the Jewish people in this time period of history that all tears were important to God. There was not one tear shed without His notice. It was a custom even to keep tears that were shed in a personal "tear bottle," and it was a sacred possession. The following Scripture verse supports that tradition with spiritual meaning.

> *You keep track of all my sorrows. You have collected all my tears in your bottle. You have recorded each one in your book. Psalm 56:8 NLT*

## Discovery Question

3. Reflect on the action of the woman as she wet the feet of Jesus with her tears and the content of Psalm 56:8. How does it make you feel that God has "kept track" of all your sorrows and "collected" all your tears in His bottle? What does it say about God's concern for you?

_____

_____

_____

_____

## Our Heart Is in the Offering

The woman brought her burdens to Jesus and placed them upon Him. She took a position of humility at His feet. She also brought a flask of perfume. It was a further tradition that such a flask was kept in a woman's dowry, to be used to anoint her husband on her wedding day. Possibly, this flask was from this woman's dowry. Whatever the reason for this perfume to be in her possession, it is clear that she anoints the feet of Lord Jesus as an act of adoration and affection. In all of her offerings, the woman is appealing to His mercy (forgiveness) and offering herself to be in relationship with Him. She is desperate for a life change. She is woman with a past. She comes with her reputation and her broken dreams. She is the lost and the least, but in Jesus she finds mercy, understanding and His redeeming power.

The Pharisee, however, is on a different page. He views the woman with contempt and consternation. She is a gross interruption and interference at his dinner party with Jesus. He even considers Jesus spiritually suspect, because He gives the woman access to Himself and receives her offerings.

> *If this man were a prophet, he would know who is touching him and what kind of woman she is—that she is a sinner. Luke 7:39*

Pharisees were part of a legalistic and separtistic group devoted to the laws of Moses and their attached *unwritten* religious traditions. Pharisees were known for their supposed "holy devotion" to the Lord. They were self-supposed "spiritual guides" for those looking for God. They considered themselves true representatives of approved Temple practice; however, they were often hypocritical. Often they were supreme examples of religion in bodily form but void of a spiritual heartbeat. That is always the danger for organized religion. True devotion to God is not in our religious form with our guarded system of order and rules. True devotion to God is in our desperate, passionate, continual reliance upon His grace and mercy. Dallas Elder *The ValueGiver p. 20–21*

## Discovery Response

⊕ From your study of the Scripture passage (Luke 7:36–50), list and compare the attitudes and reactions of the following:

The Woman

_____     _____

_____     _____

_____     _____

The Pharisee

_____     _____

_____     _____

_____     _____

Jesus

_____     _____

_____     _____

_____     _____

## Approaching the God of the Retake

People with a past often feel stuck and beyond redemption. But the truth is that they have not disqualified themselves from being redeemed, restored and having the opportunity for a meaningful future. Jesus welcomes people to bring their sins and sorrows to Him. He has a heart for the lost and the least. He is approachable and accessible. He is willing to receive our stuff and is not offended by our offerings. He is blessed to receive the alms of anguish and brokenness as an appeal for His mercy. It is a desire to change. It is a commitment of faith. It is an act of devotion. He meets our desperate approach and receives our offerings with acceptance, forgiveness, understanding and love. His approach toward us imparts worth, encourages our efforts and secures us with help and hope. He is the God of the second chance. Regardless what people have done and gone through, there is more life yet to be lived. The road of life continues from here. Jesus gives us the opportunity to begin again from where we are. Even though some people may have discarded us or pegged us into a typecast, even though we may have given up on ourselves because of our past, Jesus can redeem us from what we've been. He redeems our present and our future. Regardless of the wrong steps that we have taken, stepping toward Him enables us to take the next right step.

## Summary Response

⇒ What are some attitudes and actions that are value-giving for us and others that we will commit to employ, so that we may move beyond the poor choices of the past?

_____

_____

_____

---

**WORTH CONSIDERATION**

Sometimes we feel that the poor choices of our past have forever sidelined us from living a meaningful life of purpose and destiny. That is simply not true. We can have a new start with the help of God. Jesus invites us to bring all of our sins, sorrows and life disappointments and pour them out on Him. When we empty the distressing and disappointing contents of our heart at His feet, it illustrates our desire to be redeemed from the past for a new future. We should never let the past keep us from a new future. He invites us to come to Him, to pour out the contents of our hearts. He forgives us, accepts us and embraces us when we come. No sin is beyond His forgiveness, no life beyond His redemption.

---

# SESSION 3...*Chapter 2a*

# Re-Named for Destiny (Part One)

*Read chapter 2 (pages 27–32) of *The ValueGiver*.

**ValueGivers see personal potential and paint its portrait before unbelieving eyes. They call out destiny and risk investing in long shots. Dallas Elder *The ValueGiver p.29***

### Destiny Encounter

It is amazing how we can be living life and minding our own business when destiny dawns. While it may surprise us and may catch us off guard, inwardly we long for the encounter. There are life situations and circumstances that God uses for our destiny discovery, but most often He uses people. We could call these "divine appointments." They are not random events but God-orchestrated life scenes where we get confronted and called out into our created purpose. It is when God breaks into the routine of life and captures our attention to alert us that we have been made for something more than we have been. He assures us He instilled the longing in our hearts and birthed the dream deep within us. It is a crisis moment for us because God is calling us to be something that we desire but something we don't believe we can become. We often become afraid and filled with doubts, even withdraw from the invitation. A vision is cast that describes our heart's desire and life dream, but it is a vision difficult to embrace because we know what we have been. Qualities are called out that are stated to be within us, but that we don't see. Still, even though we may not be convinced, the One who calls us is faithful and true. He is the One who fashioned us for a purpose. Our fulfillment and destiny awaits us. The ValueGiver calls out things in us that we don't see in ourselves. He challenges us to become what we were meant to be.

A great example of a destiny encounter is found in the life of the Simon Peter. We can learn much from his relationship and interaction with Jesus so relevant to our own lives. It is an amazing journey filled with insights about ourselves and The ValueGiver.

**Scripture Reference:** Read John 1:35–42

**Discovery Question**

1. This is the first time that Jesus and Peter meet. What is the significance of Jesus' statement to Simon as it relates to him personally and to his future?

_____

_____

_____

## Destiny Reinforced

It seems that Simon Peter was shocked by Jesus' words to Him at their initial introduction. Jesus called out destiny ("rock" vision) that seemed way beyond Peter's ability. Still Jesus is persistent and pursues Peter. He goes to where Peter is and lives. He gets into his daily life and literally into his boat. When it comes to following Jesus into our destiny, often it takes some convincing. He cares enough to meet us where we are, in order to encourage us toward greater things. It is a value statement. We are worth His time. He pursues us, to enable us to get His best for our lives.

**Scripture Reference:** Read Luke 5:1–11

**Discovery Questions**

2. What is Jesus saying to Peter through the miraculous catch of fish?

_____

_____

_____

3. What do you think is in Peter's response (Luke 5:8) to Jesus?

_____

_____

_____

4. Why do you think Jesus says to Peter, "Don't be afraid" (Luke 5:10)?

_____

_____

_____

## Destiny Entanglements

Some of the difficulties in launching out when our destiny dawns are the reference points of our past failures. The call to step up to a higher plane is frightening because of all of the times we've fallen in the past. We carry the bruises of failed attempts and are ever mindful of vivid memories of disappointment. Our past experiences convince us that the future for us can be no different. So we recite the litany of "I just can't. I can't risk disappointing others and myself again." It isn't that we don't desire the destination; we just believe that it is beyond our realm of accomplishment. This is the point that Jesus made to Peter: "You have tried to do life in your own strength and failed. The call into your destiny is only possible in My strength. It is possible, but you will have to trust Me. My grace and power can transform you into all that you were meant to be."

**Scripture Reference:** Read Matthew 14:22–33

**Discovery Questions**

5.  What "destiny elements" (aspects relative to a person's destiny) are in Peter's desire and willingness to get out of the boat and walk to Jesus on the water? In other words, what were his inner motivations?

_____

_____

_____

6.  What is the response of Jesus, The ValueGiver, and what helpful principles can be gained from His response to encourage and enable people toward their destiny?

_____

_____

_____

_____

_____

_____

## The Journey to Destiny

Life is a journey. It is a challenging road, offering us a number of options and confronting us with a multitude of obstacles. We can certainly get sidetracked by detours that depart from the pathway to our purpose. Other times, we can just get stuck and settle into a rut. We begin to believe it is the limit to what we can achieve. We had hoped for more, but this seems to be where the dream ends and the vision dims. Inwardly, however, we long for more, but we become convinced of our own limitations. We may have a list of life references (disappointments, failures, etc.) that support our thinking and reinforce our "stuck" position. Peter is a wonderful example of one who has become stuck on the pathway toward his purpose. But Jesus pursues him to lift him out of the mire of life and launch him toward his destiny. It is clear that the desire for his destiny was in Peter, but it had become buried under the stuff of his life. He had concluded that he could not become who Jesus said he could be (the "rock"). But Jesus called out destiny in Peter. He invited him to trust His leadership and guidance to enable him to step out on to the pathway of his purpose. Jesus gave Peter new references points of faith to convince Peter that God has the power to make him more than he has been and enable him to do more than he has done. He cast a new vision for Peter's life. It was God's created purpose for Peter. The desire in Peter toward his destiny was being awakened and he was beginning to trust Jesus to the point that he stepped across the previous limits of his life. The ValueGiver calls out destiny in people and gives them new life reference (faith) points to help them believe for life beyond their rut.

One of the teaching means used in our lives is being invited to stretch ourselves to step out in a new direction or to try something new to gain new dimensions in life. It may seem impossible and beyond our ability. Even if we don't succeed the first time, we can learn from the experience. So much about life is learned by trial and error. It is the way children learn, it is also the way God's children learn. When we first learned to walk, we fell down some. It was part of the learning curve. If we'd never tried for fear of falling, we'd never have learned to walk. Stepping out of our rut, or our boat, at the invitation of Jesus, will be a risk, but it will open to us new dimensions of life. It will require trusting Him. We may not get it completely right the first time, but that's OK. We are taking steps out of our rut and on to the pathway to our purpose. We are gradually being transformed into the person of our destiny. The ValueGiver calls out our destiny and imparts to us courage to pursue it.

**Prayer Response**

    † Take time this week to ask the Lord to reveal to you aspects of your destiny direction. Aim for ten minutes of prayer each day. Record the destiny details revealed.

_____

_____

_____

_____

_____

_____

_____

_____

_____

_____

**WORTH CONSIDERATION**

It's unfortunate but true that we assess our future through the lens of our past. To consider becoming more than we've been is desirable and exciting, but also frightening. Inwardly we desire destiny moments and strategic encounters with people who offer us opportunities for personal growth and life advancement. But we also hear a chorus of negative voices within us saying, "That's not who you are." "You could never do that, or be that." "That's way beyond your capacity." Then vivid scenes of past-life episodes flash through our minds that lend convincing support to the disparaging statements. Our vision for life can be cast by the failures of our past. We will veto the offer for a glorious future based on that evidence. We become convinced that we cannot change. There can be nothing better for us. We will always be who we've always been. But it's simply not true. The ValueGiver, Jesus, offers us a life of purpose beyond our past. He sees more in us than we see in ourselves. Change is possible. The question is, will we trust Him and follow Him on the pathway to greater purpose, our created Kingdom contribution, increased life satisfaction and destiny fulfillment?

# Session 4…*Chapter 2b*

# Re-Named for Destiny (Part Two)

*Read chapter 2 (pages 33–47) of *The ValueGiver*.

**It is supremely important for you to believe in God. It is equally important for you to know that God believes in you.**
**Dallas Elder**

### Encouragement: The Difference Maker

I'm not sure that we have fully realized how powerful encouragement is. It is truly *value investment*. Encouragement identifies the good stuff in us and draws it out into the world to benefit the lives of others and, as well, our own. It's like a scanner that reveals gifts, skills and strengths within us but that are hidden beneath the surface. It's like a probe that releases hidden potential. It is a "worth statement" that says, "You have much to offer and more than you've previously known." It is an expression of love and concern that calls us to rise up to the fullness of life. Encouragement enables us to reach heights of life, achievement and personal development that cannot be reached without it. It is the "difference maker" for destinies.

**Scripture Reference:** Read Matthew 16:13–20

**Discovery Questions**

1.  In what ways did Jesus encourage Peter?

    _____

    _____

    _____

2.  How do you think Jesus' words of encouragement spoke specifically to Peter's destiny?

    _____

    _____

    _____

**Scripture Reference:** Read Matthew 16:21–23

**Discovery Question**

3.  How do you think Peter could be on the mark with Jesus in the previous conversation (Matthew 16:13–20) and miss the mark with Jesus in this interchange?

_____

_____

_____

## Caring Enough to Correct

Constructive correction is an expression of encouragement and a teaching tool. Jesus employs it here with Peter. It is also a deeper investment into the relationship and Peter's development toward his destiny. ValueGivers are not "done" with people if they miss the mark. They tenderly help them to see their mistakes and learn from them.

> ValueGivers care enough to correct and don't get exasperated when people miss the mark. They are willing to ride the roller coaster of the learning curve. They stay plugged into the relationship in order to speak the necessary adjustments crucial to the person's development and destiny. Dallas Elder *The ValueGiver p.36*

## Affirmation before Failure

> *Simon, Simon, Satan has asked to sift you like wheat. But I have prayed for you, that your faith may not fail. And when you have turned back, strengthen your brothers. Luke 22:31–32a*

Jesus spoke to Peter with prophetic insight when He told him he was going to fall into temptation and deny that he even knew Jesus (Luke 22:54b–63). While it was going to be a failure and a devastating disappointment for Peter, Jesus was letting him know that He would still be with Peter on the other side of the dark experience. In other words, their relationship would continue. ValueGivers hang with people through their failures. This is a necessary redemptive effort that enables people to be restored and reengage the pathway toward their purpose on the other side of the valley of despair. It is a tenacious love and grace embrace that commits to walk with people through the times in their lives when they are not at their best. The action does not condone the wrong doing or poor choice. The ValueGiver covenant simply says, "I love you, I believe in you and I am committed to you for the long haul. There will be valleys on the journey toward your destiny. I will walk with you through the valley and never abandon you there."

Too often people have been left and lost in the valley of disgrace. It is where they're stuck and they can't get out on their own. They have disappointed themselves and the people they care about. But the fact is that the pathway of purpose and destiny continues on the other side of the valley. There is more life to be lived and they have not disqualified themselves from their destiny. Jesus affirmed His relationship and commitment to Peter on the front side of the failure. He did so to convince Peter that the journey toward his destiny would continue beyond the valley and that Jesus was committed to walk it out with him.

**Scripture Reference:** Read Mark 16:6–7

**Discovery Questions**

4. In these instructions given by the angel to the women, why do you think Peter's name is specifically mentioned?

_____

_____

5. What does this say about Jesus and His relationship with Peter and with us?

_____

_____

_____

## Restoration and Recovery

No doubt following his failure, Peter felt devastated and disqualified from the destiny that Jesus had called for him. He sinks back into the old familiar life he had always known. This is the default mode for most people. But Jesus goes and finds Peter, in order to restore him and recover his destiny.

**Scripture Reference:** Read John 21:1–19

**Discovery Questions**

6. What is the significance of Jesus' questions and Peter's responses? What did this do for Peter?

_____

_____

_____

_____

_____

7. How was this counseling session with Jesus paramount for Peter's destiny?

_____

_____

_____

## Summary Response

⇒ What are two things you learned or became more aware of through the study of the last two sessions (over chapter 2)? What is one thing relative to this teaching you are going to give attention to in your life?

_____

_____

_____

_____

_____

_____

---

**WORTH CONSIDERATION**
Failure is never permanent. Failure does not define us. Failure describes an unsuccessful attempt. It's over. New situations await us, which are opportunities for different results. We must learn from our failures. Successes are built upon them. We will not always get it right. God knows. He will use our failures as a learning curve. He will not give up on us. It is important that we do not give up on ourselves. Continue to trust and follow Jesus through the maze of mistakes.

---

**Note:** To get moving on the pathway to our purpose, it is important for us to work through our failures. The addendum in the back of *The ValueGiver* has been provided to assist people to get out of the valley and, with God's help, get on their destiny road. The last session of this study guide (Session 13) is designed to help lead you through this redeeming, healing, freeing and positioning process.

# SESSION 5...*Chapter 3*

# Trial Offers

*Read chapter 3 of *The ValueGiver*.

**Different worlds have different riches. Valuing, rather than discounting and distancing ourselves from challenges and challenged people, alerts us to gems they possess which have the capacity to enrich our lives.  Dallas Elder *The ValueGiver* p.59**

### The Thing about Trials

Something that is common to all of us in life is that we are going to encounter trials. While these times of trouble, challenge and struggle are stressful and difficult, they are a part of life. No one living in our world is immune to trials. Sometimes it has been thought that those who have faith in God will not encounter trouble. It's also been thought that only the unrighteous experience trouble. Jesus said, "In this world you will have trouble." (John 16:33) No doubt all of us would like to position ourselves to have a trouble-free life, but the truth is that everyone will face trials. It is also true that they serve a significant purpose in our lives.

Suffering trials can leave us with the impression that there must be something wrong with us. They can seem to be a gross injustice. They can cause us to question the love and protection of God. Our troubles become another evil source to strip away our self-worth. They are enemies to our existence. Because trials are so distasteful, we distance ourselves from them at all costs. In doing so, we also distance ourselves from people going through challenges, leaving them alone and stigmatized. To support a person in their hour of crisis is a powerful value statement. Understanding the nature of trials will help us deepen our faith and understanding of God, as well as our compassion for others.

**Scripture Reference:** Read James 1:2–8

**Discovery Questions**

1.  What should be our attitude and approach to the trials we encounter?

_____

_____

_____

2. What benefits are mentioned in this passage that may be gained through our times of trial?

_____

_____

_____

_____

_____

_____

## Sources of Trials

It is possible for us to afflict ourselves with trials. Our choices and actions always have consequences. So our poor choices can certainly be a source of our difficulties. We have all been there one time or another. Hopefully we learn from our mistakes and minimize our afflictions by making wiser decisions in the future. There are three other sources of trials mentioned in the whole of Scripture.

## Discovery Questions

3. What are the three sources of trials mentioned in chapter 3 of *The ValueGiver*? Give a brief explanation of each.

   ➢ _____

_____

_____

   ➢ _____

_____

_____

   ➢ _____

_____

_____

4. Reflect upon a challenging situation (trial) that you have encountered. What were some valuable insights or lessons about faith and life you learned through the experience?

_____

_____

_____

_____

## Trial Opportunities

Trials serve as windows into our world to view wonderful new vistas of perspective and to gain knowledge about faith, life, ourselves and others, which simply cannot be gained any other way. It is a difficult road but one full of enriching discoveries. Through tribulations, our lives are refined and defined. Our character is shaped and our faith is strengthened. While they have the harsh appearance of robbing us of life, God uses them to give us great gains. Trials afford the opportunity to show compassion to those who are suffering. They bring us to a crossroads of choosing, to distance ourselves from others in need of help or, to engage them to support them in their day of crisis. Trials temper our mercy.

**Scripture Reference:** Read Luke 10:25–37

**Discovery Question**

5. List the differences you see between the attitudes and actions of the priest and Levite verses that of the Samaritan to the man in crisis.

_____

_____

_____

_____

## Action beyond Abandonment

The way that we respond to people going through trials speaks volumes about the content of our heart. Often people mercilessly criticize or judge people in the moments of their misfortune. At other times the reaction is to avoid or abandon the person experiencing a difficult time. It is a fair-weather friend who is a friend only in the good times. All of us will encounter hard times at some point. Trials are a natural part of life. We can count on The ValueGiver to always be with us in our difficult moments and to help us through them. "A friend loves at all times...." (Proverbs 17:17). "...there is a friend who sticks closer than a brother" (Proverbs

18:24). Jesus, The ValueGiver, is such a friend. When we offer attention and assistance to people in life crisis, we communicate to them that they are not alone or abandoned in their dark hour. Standing with them and helping the one going through a fierce trial conveys worth. It says, "You matter." It births hope and can literally be the difference between life or death, victory or defeat. The compassionate action preserves the person and positions them for life beyond their present trouble. Note the value-giving and supportive reputation of Job as a responder to people in crisis as revealed in the Scripture verse below.

> *Your words have supported those who stumbled; you have strengthened faltering knees. Job 4:4 NIV*

> *Your words have put stumbling people on their feet, put fresh hope in people about to collapse. Job 4:4 The Message*

## Summary Response

⇒ Has there been a time someone came to you in your hour of trouble and helped you stand and helped strengthen you to make it through? If so, what was the crisis and what was one helpful thing they did for you?

_____

_____

_____

⇒ Based on the teaching in this lesson, what is one thing that sticks out to you that you will work on to employ in your life?

_____

_____

_____

---

**WORTH CONSIDERATION**

When we go through difficult times, trials and tribulations, we can get the idea that something must be wrong with us. Evil tells us we deserve it. We may even believe that we live under a curse. No doubt, we can create our own problems, but trials are normal and even necessary in life. They will grow us as persons and strengthen our faith. We need to look for the treasures in the trials, trust that God will always sustain us, and be considerate of others overwhelmed by distressing situations. Crisis feels very depreciating. The mercy and support we offer values people and gives them hope as they walk through the valley of despair.

---

# SESSION 6…*Chapter 4*

# Transforming Trolls

*Read chapter 4 of *The ValueGiver*.

## I WILL CHANGE YOUR NAME
### Song by D. J. Butler

**I will change your name
You shall no longer be called
Wounded, outcast
Lonely or afraid**

**I will change your name
Your new name shall be
Confident, joyfulness,
Overcoming one,
Faithfulness, Friend of God
One who seeks My face.[2]**

### A Name Changer

There's often a certain point in a sporting event when a specific play changes the course of the game. It is a difference maker. It directs the outcome from defeat to victory. It's called a "game changer." The ValueGiver is a "name changer." He transforms labels that have been hung on people due to their misfortune, stereotype in society, sullied reputation and so on. Names are powerful. They peg people in their perceived position in the world. Names are life descriptions and often life prescriptions. In other words, our lives unfold from our labels.

It seems that the world likes labels. Life labels allow people to be categorized and, unfortunately, stigmatized. People are pegged in their place. With their place comes an assessed value and stature in society. Often people are "put in their place" based on the way they're born. Do people meet the eye test? Appearance may be a factor. Race or ethnicity may be a factor. Socio-economics may be a factor. Historical prejudice may be a factor. The way certain people or people groups are generally viewed in the region may be a factor. The point is that there are factors, working constructs, in the world used to describe, define and categorize people in their place. This renders an assessment of their worth in the world. The assessment can be totally false and skewed by the distorted views of society, but still it pegs a person with a stigma that is difficult to shake. It does something else that is equally damaging to one's personhood. The category they have been assigned comes with a ceiling that limits potential and personal advancement. Once you're labeled, you're labeled. Once you're named, you're named. Once you're pegged, you're pegged for life. How unjust and unfair!

Jesus, The ValueGiver, has a different valuing system. He does not assign value to people based on how they were born, the judgments of society or past reputations. He offers to us fair-market value, the fullness of God's created intention for us. He positions us in a redeemed category, primed to reach our personal potential, fulfill our purpose and complete our destiny. His grace and power can break us out of our life label, category and confinement. He can give us a new name for a new future. He is a "name changer."

**Scripture Reference:** Read Luke 19:1–10

**Discovery Question**

1. What were the life challenges Zacchaeus was facing?

_____

_____

_____

_____

2. How do you think these challenges affected his view of himself? How do you think they could have affected his view of God?

_____

_____

_____

_____

_____

_____

### Dealing with a Bad Hand

Sometimes life deals us a bad hand. It is a misfortune or injustice beyond our control that we are forced to deal with. It is beyond the norm of those around us and moves us into a challenged minority. We may wonder *Why me?* or *Why,*

*God?* There may be reactions to us because we are different than the norm due to our challenge. We may certainly feel different, even ostracized and may feel that we don't belong. Our challenge may even make us question God's love and concern for us. Inwardly, it is natural to question our worth and wonder if we really have a purpose. Our life challenges and unfortunate experiences can affect us both socially and spiritually.

## Discovery Questions

3. Have you had a life challenge or experience that has made you feel different than the norm? If so, briefly explain:

_____

_____

_____

4. How did your experience affect your view of yourself? How did it affect your view of God?

_____

_____

_____

_____

_____

_____

### The Redeemer's Response

Jesus came into the town of Jericho and was met by huge crowds in the street. He came directly to where Zacchaeus was perched in a tree to catch a glimpse of Him. Jesus spoke to him and insisted that He should come to Zacchaeus's home. The gracious approach and words of Jesus spoke volumes of value to the rejected man and led to his redemption and to that of his family.

## Discovery Question

5. Examine the interaction between Jesus and Zacchaeus, beginning at the sycamore tree and concluding in the home (Luke 19:5–9). What are the value-giving traits that can be identified in Jesus' approach (actions) and words to Zacchaeus?

_____

_____

_____

_____

_____

_____

## The Religious Response

*All the people saw this and began to mutter, He has gone to be the guest of a 'sinner.'* Luke 19:7

The response of the religious establishment toward Zacchaeus was less than gracious. Rather than viewing Zacchaeus's encounter with Jesus as encouraging, it was viewed with consternation. Sometimes religious people in the faith community, or church, have been less than accepting or affirming to people with certain issues. These "religious" attitudes and their assigned labels can hinder people from coming to faith and certainly keeps them at a distance from the faith community. They deem certain people as outcasts and beyond the reach of God's grace. This stereotyping makes the victims feel worthless and hopeless. These merciless types of religious attitudes resurface in every generation.

### Discovery Question

6. What are some attitudes or approaches you could change that would help people to feel more welcome into the faith community?

_____

_____

_____

_____

### Summary Response

⇒ Attitude adjustment: Has there been a less-than-gracious religious attitude God has dealt with or is dealing with in you? If so, what is it?

_____

⇒ Attitude abuse: Was there a time you were the victim of unrighteous religious attitudes? Describe.

_____

_____

_____

_____

**WORTH CONSIDERATION**

Labels are so confining and hard to shake. They can be like a die that's cast. They come from prejudices in society, cold categorizations from merciless people and sometimes from our own self-assessment. It becomes a name that describes us. We live under the label. In many ways, it is a name we're called by and answer to. It becomes an intrinsic part of our identity. Often we've had no choice in the matter or in what the world calls us. It's been like our chosen lot, a crude stroke of fate. The good news is that The ValueGiver is a name changer. Though the world handed us one label, He stands ready to offer us a new one. A label change can mean a life change. We can chart a new course and become a new person. We can see ourselves differently. We begin to think differently. We begin to emerge into the description of the new name. God's affirmation of us, as His children, creates a new identity of confidence, courage and limitless possibilities.

# SESSION 7...*Chapter 5*

# Crossing Lines

*Read chapter 5 of *The ValueGiver.*

**The Church is central to God's plan to redeem the world. The Church, the followers of Jesus throughout the world, collectively making up the Body of Christ, is a relational, incarnational representation of Jesus and His ministry. At its best, it reflects the love, passion, transformational truth and power of Christ. It is a force to usher in the Kingdom of God into the earthly landscape of every generation, proclaiming the way of salvation for all peoples. It is a hope-filled, life-giving, healing, freeing community that welcomes and nurtures the helpless and hurting, the derelict and disenfranchised. At its worst, it offers empty rituals, pious platitudes, self-serving purposes and impotent activities. It builds more barriers than bridges in its task to redeem the world. Dallas Elder *The ValueGiver p.80***

**Scripture References:** Read John 2:13–17

*Is it not written: 'My house will be called a house of prayer for the nations'? But you have made it a 'den of robbers.' Mark 11:17*

**Discovery Questions**

1.  Why is Jesus so upset?  Are you surprised?

_____

_____

_____

2.  From your observation of the Scripture passage (John 2:13–17) and your reading of chapter 5 in *The ValueGiver*, what were the inappropriate misrepresentation issues of the temple (the church)?

_____

_____

_____

_____

_____

## Indignant Demolition

This episode in the life and times of Jesus has often surprised people. For some it seems out of character. The passive, meek and mild Jesus aggressively turned over the tables of the money changers and drove them out of the temple with a whip. At first glance, He may have appeared as a man who snapped, created a spectacle, and who, with His temper out of control, was having a really bad day.

No doubt Jesus was ticked off. The atmosphere in the sanctuary of His Father's house had the appearance of a worldly, self-serving marketplace. Not only was that a gross misrepresentation of its true purpose, but it took advantage of humble people and made it difficult for them to find authentic faith and worship God. The house of God was functioning more like the game show, *Let's Make a Deal*, than the house of prayer it was intended to be. Among the several inappropriate issues in the temple were the "approved" self-serving practices of the marketers and the barriers they were creating for people with sincere hearts who were genuinely trying to get to God.

So the indignant Jesus, with righteous passion for His Father's house, began cleaning house. It was not the tirade of a spoiled child. It was a necessary correction to strip away the inauthentic and self-serving, to restore the temple's true heart and strategic purpose for the authentic representation of God to the people of the world. Jesus passionately wanted His Father's house to serve His Father's purpose.

## Religion: A Self-Serving System

What Jesus was clearing from the floor of the temple was just surface debris from a much deeper problem. True worship of God had become a self-serving religious system. People who came to worship God fell prey to the schemes of the temple "business," the money changers and such. It made it difficult for people seeking God to get to Him. The house of God had become a house of crooked commerce. It was a gross misrepresentation of God's intention and functioning far from His purpose. So Jesus cleaned house to restore His Father's purpose for His Father's house. Jesus modeled by His life the Kingdom principle of serving others.

**Discovery Question**

3.  In this present generation, what are the prejudices and barriers that make it difficult for people to be welcome, to find God and to belong to the faith community?

_____

_____

_____

_____


**Scripture Reference:** Read John 13:12–17

**Discovery Question**

4.  From the previous passage of Scripture, what is the *example* that Jesus is teaching His disciples? Elaborate.

_____

_____

_____

_____


## The Transformed Temple

What began with Jesus "cleaning house" ended with Jesus establishing a new order of worship. Religion is a self-serving, man-manufactured system that has the surface appearance of spirituality but in reality is empty ritual, a misrepresentation of the true heart of God and exclusionary toward certain people. Jesus came as the Redeemer of all mankind. He came into the world to become our Savior by dying for our sins. He also came to transform His "temple" and establish His Church as a true representation of the heart of God with its members worshipping God in spirit and in truth. It is a place of grace and welcome for all people. Everyone has equal access to God and opportunity to worship and serve Him without the confinements of prejudice.

**Scripture Reference:** Read Matthew 27:50–53

**Discovery Question**

5. From reading this passage and referencing *The ValueGiver* (pages 88–89), what is the significance of the curtain being torn? What did it mean for the people of the world?

_____

_____

_____

_____

The conclusion of the temple transformation took place in Acts chapter 2, when the Holy Spirit came to the followers of Jesus who had gathered for prayer. The departing words of Jesus, before He ascended to Heaven following His resurrection were to "wait for the Holy Spirit." The "Temple," or Church of God, is not a building; it is His people in worship and living in obedience to Him. There was a stark contrast between the self-serving religious establishment conducting business in the temple, which Jesus cleared, and the Church Jesus was establishing.

**Scripture Reference:** Read Acts 2:43–47

**Discovery Question**

6. Note the contrast between the attitudes and activities of the temple that Jesus cleared and the attitudes and activities of the new and transformed Temple/Church that was emerging as represented in the above passage. What are the contrasting differences that you see between the two?

| **Temple** | **Transformed Temple** |
| --- | --- |
| _____ | _____ |
| _____ | _____ |
| _____ | _____ |
| _____ | _____ |
| _____ | _____ |

**Summary Response**

⇒ What is one new thing you have learned through the study of chapter 5 in *The ValueGiver*?

_____

⇒ How will it be lived out in awareness or application in your life?

_____

_____

_____

---

**WORTH CONSIDERATION**

Jesus intends His Church to be a place where people are welcome, accepted and encouraged to find faith. When relationship with God is turned into a religious system of ritual, routines and self-serving efforts, it becomes empty of the presence and purposes of God. Man gets in the way of God. It makes genuine faith, spiritual connection and community difficult. Front and center are the self-serving activities of people and lost is the true representation of who God is. People genuinely seeking relationship with God become distracted and disillusioned. The Church is to represent God's heart and compassion, composed of authentic people offering authentic faith to help others experience the kindness of God. We need to build bridges and not barriers for people to come to know God. When we do so, people come to believe that they are valued by God.

# SESSION 8...*Chapter 6*

# Moving Fences

*Read chapter 6 of *The ValueGiver*.

**All values in this world are more or less questionable, but the most important thing in life is human kindness.[3]**
**Yevgeny Yevtushenko**

### The Prejudice Ploy

Prejudice says, "You don't get to be in the circle. You don't make the team. You don't get to play." It's all judgment—not on the basis of your skill, your ability or giftedness, but on the basis of how you were born. The list is long for excluding people. People aren't the right race, the right gender, or live on the right side of the street. People have 'pasts' and therefore don't qualify to get a shot at the future. It is amazing how often we give such people a permanently assessed value. Dallas Elder *The ValueGiver p.94*

Prejudice is one of the great depreciating spirits in any culture or society. It steals away worth and lowers self-esteem. It erects barriers, confines advancement, assigns people limited social space and assigns people a less-than value. It does not afford people equal opportunity. There maybe numerous motives underlying the prejudice ploy, but there is a common theme: "I deem you beneath me." It is certainly a depreciating value statement.

Prejudice exists in every culture and every generation in one form or another. Sometimes it is very overt, other times it is very subtle. None the less, it labels people, puts them in categories and it builds fences to confine people in their stereotyped roles in society. It gives the ruling class, the favored cast, the select club, a seemingly greater value. They appear superior because they make others inferior. It is a corrupt, self-serving practice and depreciating social system. Prejudice can be views and values handed down through our family, instituted by society and reinforced by tradition. At times, it is perpetuated by the Church. We learn the bigoted ways as natural to life, and they shape us. We become "carriers" into our generation and model them for the next.

**Discovery Questions**

1. Has there been an instance in your life when you were the subject of prejudice or witnessed acts of prejudice toward others? Describe.

_____

_____

_____

_____

2. How did the prejudice reaction or experience make you feel?

_____

_____

_____

**Scripture Reference:** Read Acts 10:1–9

### Acceptance Adjustment

God had people that He desired to reach for His Kingdom and enfold into His family. Peter was a leader in His Church and an intended representative of His grace and truth. But Peter was a product of his culture and social structure that held prejudice bents toward certain people groups, specifically the Romans. Peter had personally received a life change through the grace of the Savior Jesus Christ. He was a committed follower and prominent minister in His emerging Church. But Peter held views toward certain people groups that narrowed his vision and blocked the extension of God's grace toward these individuals. So God had to do an acceptance adjustment in Peter's heart and reprogram his biased thinking. Otherwise, the social barriers propped up by prejudice would continue to limit the communication of the gospel and severely shorten the loving reach of God's saving grace toward all people.

The Jews were proud of their heritage as God's chosen race. Peter was a Jew, but he had come to full salvation through faith in the saving work of Jesus on the cross, which brought the forgiveness of sins and new life through the Holy Spirit. While Peter was wonderfully saved by grace, he still held to a prideful prejudice and spiritual elitism that kept him at a distance from the Gentiles. They had unclean practices that weren't acceptable for Jews. It was considered holy to keep the distance and the discriminating barriers in place. But God was building a bridge of redemption to reach them. Peter was a pillar of God's Church. He had to blow up Peter's old bias boxes, in order to enlarge his heart and use him to offer to all people, God's grace embrace.

### Discovery Questions

3. Why was it important for Peter to receive God's acceptance adjustment?

_____

_____

_____

4. Peter struggled with completely changing his mindset and relapsed into his discriminating thinking (Galatians 2:11–13). Why, do you believe, prejudices run so deep in the layers of our lives?

_____

_____

_____

5. What are ways we limit people through our prejudicial views toward them?

_____

_____

_____

### Arrows Aimed at Acceptance

Let's get personal for a moment. Allow for this "acceptance interlude" of inward inspection of your own self-acceptance level relative to your self-image. Acceptance arrows (devilish darts targeted to deflate your self-acceptance) are crooked, sharp, jaded statements, messages, life experiences, personal failures, injustices and abuses that are intentionally or unintentionally aimed at your self-image. (They can be self-inflicted wounds.) Your soul and inner-being are their targets. Evil forces assist in loading the venomous arrows into quivers, aim them at the core of your being, launch the flaming darts and pierce your inner person. They release infectious shame, guilt, inadequacy, inferiority and a sense of being unworthy and unacceptable. It's amazing and true that we respond to others out of the content of our personal core. When we can identify the arrows that damage and diminish our self-image and self-acceptance, we can hand those over to Jesus. He will stop the bleeding, heal the wounds and restore us to wholeness. Our sense of acceptance is a measure of personal worth. It is out of this well that we measure out cups of worth to others through our responses and reactions.

### Discovery Question

6. What are specific examples of arrows aimed at diminishing a person's self-acceptance and self-image? It may be helpful for you to identify and reference "arrows" that have wounded you.

_____

_____

_____

_____

_____

_____

_____

### Redemptive Keys

People can get locked down beneath their poor choices, bad reputations and cultural stigmas. Our prejudices and biases toward certain sins and certain people can cause us to view these certain people beyond redemption. Often the prejudicial views of religious people that wall out certain types of people are supported by a limited knowledge of the Scripture and a distorted view of God. This combines for a faulty theology and a minimizing faith. (For instance, for centuries the Church, by and large, supported slavery and reinforced its view from the Bible. History is full of episodes where the status quo masses justified limiting the rights, freedoms and opportunities of specific people groups.) Bigoted mindsets and narrow thinking keep certain people on the other side of the fence and deny them the invitation to receive God's saving grace and equal value.

For us to be fully usable as God's representatives of His love and redemption unilaterally to all people, God has to break down our biased categories and prejudiced stereotypes. He gives us new revelation through a broader understanding of His passionate heart for redeeming all people. He gives us a deeper understanding of His Word, which reveals His mercy toward the whole of mankind. He corrects our flawed thinking and theology to include everyone as objects of His love, acceptance and forgiveness. This greater "grace revelation" not only enlarges our hearts toward those who we kept on the other side of the fence, but it enables us to experience God's grace more deeply in our own lives. We continue to be awed by His amazing grace in our hearts. We receive the effects of His mercy and love, which lifts us up to new levels of assurance and faith.

### Summary Response

⇒ Summarize the significance and meaning of the following statement: "We have thought and taught that people need to believe in order to belong, but people need to belong in order to believe." (George Hunter)

_____

_____

_____

_____

_____

_____

_____

_____

**WORTH CONSIDERATION**

God often has to do an acceptance work in our hearts so that we can offer His grace and acceptance to others. When we feel that we have been placed on the other side of the fence, we tend to categorize people in similar ways due to our self-acceptance deficit. Removing the arrows from our own heart, helps us own prejudicial issues. It prevents us continuing to build walls of separation and from being used by evil to launch infectious arrows targeting certain people to inflict hurt and diminish their worth. When we have truly received God's grace and acceptance for our own souls, we can genuinely lead with it to embrace and accept others. Rather than erecting fences of exclusion, we mend fences for inclusion. His love within us arcs over barriers to embrace others, redeem them and include them in the faith community. The keys of redemption are generated out of God's love for all people. The redemptive keys are acceptance, forgiveness and an invitation to belong. This is the grace embrace that invites people to be redeemed for the full value of their created worth. As followers of Jesus Christ, we hold the keys of redemption.

# SESSION 9...*Chapter 7*

# Possessing Poor Vision

*Read chapter 7 of *The ValueGiver*.

**God's guest list includes a disconcerting number of poor and broken people, those who appear to bring little to any gathering except their need. The distinctive quality of Christian hospitality is that it offers a generous welcome to the "least," without concern for advantage or benefit to the host. Such hospitality reflects God's greater hospitality that welcomes the undeserving, provides the lonely with a home, and sets a banquet table for the hungry....Hospitality is central to the meaning of the gospel.[4] Christine Pohl**

### More than Tolerant

Jesus had room in His heart and His life for the poor. He modeled, through His attitude and actions, how to respond to the less fortunate. He valued them as human beings and gave them equal respect. He did not consider them the scourge of the earth or a waste of His time. They were neither invisible nor insignificant. They were just people struggling in life and requiring attention and assistance when the situation called for it. He taught His followers to be alert to the needs of the poor and to dignify the poor person. Jesus indicated that our reaction and response toward the poor speaks volumes about the spiritual content of our heart.

It is easy for the poor to become invisible in society. We can become bothered by their conditions, their neediness and misfortune, while we become prideful in our own good fortune. The poor carry a stigma from which we want to distance ourselves. In doing so, we galvanize ourselves from people living in the dregs of poverty. We begin to train ourselves just to look the other way. There is disgust with the despicable elements of their lifestyle and an urge within us to disassociate. We direct our gaze away from their plight and remove ourselves from any sense of concern.  In no way do we want to feel any obligation to help.

Jesus taught that the poor were to be more than tolerated in a society; they were to be embraced in our society. Rather than looking down on the poor and disassociating with the needy as outcasts, Jesus elevated them as an object of His compassion.

**Scripture Reference:** Luke 14:12–14

**Discovery Questions**

1. Examining this statement of Jesus, what was the most common and usual practice of people regarding who they invite into their lives?

_____

_____

_____

2. What is Jesus advocating as the Christian response toward the poor, disabled and less fortunate?

_____

_____

_____

3. What attitudes have you held toward the poor?

_____

_____

_____

4. If you have held attitudes that have led you to disassociate yourself from the poor, what has been the basis of these attitudes? In other words, how did these attitudes develop in your life?

_____

_____

_____

_____

_____

### Connecting Our Vision to Our Heart

People do not see what they do not value. Jesus was raising the awareness of the poor in the vision scope of His followers. People become detached and even desensitized to the disturbing and unpleasant conditions of others. Jesus teaches us that the poor are to be valued and embraced. They need to have a place in our hearts. There needs to be compassion and concern for them as people God loves. There are ways that all of us have been poor and needy. We have needed God's mercy and the compassionate assistance of others to get through the difficult stretches of our lives. We need to remember the merciful help God has given us that has often come to us through the kindness of others in undeserved ways. It is amazing how quickly we can forget the mercy of God and the kindness of others that came to our aid at a desperate time.

To be alert to the needs of the less fortunate God brings within the scope of our vision and concern, indicates that we have not forgotten the mercy, kindness and undeserved aid God has given us. We remember that there were human heart and hands, which were His instruments, that displayed His aid and that helped us through our difficult times. God's heart for the poor is reflected and demonstrated through His followers. They are not forgotten to Him and they should not be forgotten to us. As we carry within us the active reminder of His mercy to us, we share an active concern for others in need of His kindness. We see their needs. We see them as people. We are moved with compassion, which results in acts of kindness that aid their circumstances.

The call of the Church of Jesus Christ is to "**remember the poor**."

**Scripture Reference:** Read Galatians 2:9–10

> 5. What are some of the difficulties you have considered or observed in embracing and serving the needs of the poor?

_____

_____

_____

_____

_____

### Embracing the Poor, Embracing Jesus

As we read through the Scripture, we find that the poor are more than a causal concern. As jarring as it may sound, our attitude toward the less fortunate is "heart-wired" to our relationship with God. To have a heart for Jesus means that we hold His concerns within us and reflect those in our lives. Our devotion to Christ is illustrated through worship, prayer, tithes and offerings, and obedience to His commandments, but it is also illustrated by serving the needs of others. To detach and distance ourselves from the less fortunate is to detach and distance ourselves from Christ. He so identifies Himself with the needy that He says that when we touch them, we touch Him. He emphasizes to us that serving the needs of the poor is an important part of our devotion and reflects a depth of commitment to Him. Our devotion to Christ is demonstrated in our sensitivity, concern and practical assistance.

As James reminds us, genuine compassion is demonstrated in deeds.

> *Suppose a brother or sister is without clothes and daily food. If one of you says to him, "Go, I wish you well; keep warm and well fed," but does nothing about his physical needs, what good is it? In the same way, faith by itself, if it is not accompanied by action, is dead. James 2:15–17*

Jesus emphasizes to us that by serving the poor that we are personally serving Him. In other words, He takes our attitudes and actions toward the poor very personally. As we do unto them, so we do unto Him. When we touch them, we touch Him.

**Scripture Reference:** Read Matthew 25:31–46

**Discovery Question**

6. What are the attitudes and actions toward the poor that reflect the heart of Jesus and genuine Christian faith you have learned through your study of this lesson? List them below.

| Attitudes | Actions |
|-----------|---------|
| _____ | _____ |
| _____ | _____ |
| _____ | _____ |
| _____ | _____ |
| _____ | _____ |
| _____ | _____ |

**Summary Response**

⇒ Share insights you learned about yourself and about the Christian response to the poor. In your summary response include one thing you will keep in mind as you have opportunity to interact with the less fortunate.

_____

_____

_____

_____

_____

_____

_____

_____

**WORTH CONSIDERATION**

We need to have a place in our hearts and lives for the poor and disenfranchised. We need to make room for them. The application of this will look different for all of us. But there should be a dedicated portion of time, effort and resources invested as situations arise. Neglect of the poor will cripple our Christian walk. Investing in the poor is a significant expression of devotion to Christ. It honors Him as we honor those who are less fortunate with compassion and concern.

# SESSION 10...*Chapter 8*

# Hope Beyond Hopeless

*Read chapter 8 of *The ValueGiver*.

**Grace is the empowering Presence of God that enables us to be what God has called us to be.[5] Gary Smalley**

### The Grace Gaze

It is the grace of God that enables us to arise from beneath our brokenness and bondage and become the divine design of God's intended creation. Each of us has been created with a purpose. Through the dysfunctional stuff of our lives, the true person gets buried under the garbage. Our vision of ourselves and our hope for a better future is distorted and dashed, because we are covered up by piles of junk. God's "grace gaze" peers through our broken stuff and identifies the person beneath the layers of dysfunction and distortion. He reaches into the trash heap and draws us out. He speaks to us the true vision of who He created us to be. His grace and heavenly help enables us to become that person.

When we look at other people through the lens of grace, we begin to see the real person beneath the disturbing, dysfunctional and destructive behavior. Some people are helplessly and hopelessly trapped in their trash. They've tried by their own strength to escape. Others with good intentions have tried to assist. Unfortunately, they remain stuck in their stuff. They appear to be hopeless. The grace gaze sees beyond hopeless. It sees the true person and the potential that God sees in them. The grace gaze casts a vision of redemption, restoration and hope. It initiates a work of God that redeems the person for their intended purpose, a life beyond what they've been living.

**Scripture Reference:** Read Mark 5:1–17

**Discovery Questions**

1. What are the elements present in this passage that reinforce the hopelessness of this man?

   _____

   _____

2.  For what reasons do you think people tend to "give up" on challenged people and deem them as hopeless causes?

_____

_____

_____

_____

_____

3.  What things do you see in Jesus' attitude and approach toward the demonized man that illustrates a redemptive pathway to help the hopeless?

_____

_____

_____

_____

_____

### Life beyond No Hope

Often people who are engulfed in challenging circumstances are considered beyond hope. Their condition is reinforced by their futile attempts to help themselves. Their situation is further exacerbated by the failed attempts of good-intentioned others, sometimes even professionals. It is good and genuine help but it has no effect. The person appears hopelessly stuck in this life slot with no recourse. All rescue attempts have failed. He or she remains in the death grip of their dysfunction, which is so intense, it drives away even people who genuinely care for them. Their life is out of control, dangerous and destructive. Evil reigns over them and has bound them with unbreakable chains. Those who have made their "helpful" attempts have become exasperated and have given up. Others keep at a distance due to fear and caution. Based upon these reference points, the person is deemed beyond hope.

When self-effort and the ingenuity of man have been ineffective, there is another approach that remains. There is the power of prayer that initiates the intervention of God. The help of God is greater than the help of man. As dark, dismal and dysfunctional as a person may be, God can break their chains of bondage. After prayerful preparation and discerning the steps to take, the ValueGiver will make an approach to the helpless and hopeless person in the grace, truth and power of Jesus. He is the hope of the hopeless. The light is always more powerful than the darkness. How unfortunate when people are written off as hopeless!

The Father led Jesus to pause what He was doing, get in a boat and go to the other side of the Sea of Galilee. It was there that He brought God's help to a helpless and hopeless man, living among the tombs and consumed in destructive behavior. He loved, valued and approached the demonic man. He redeemed him and restored him for a supreme purpose. Though others wrote the crazy man off as hopeless, God saw him as redeemable. And by the power of God, he was redeemed.

**Scripture Reference:** Read Mark 5:18–20

**Discovery Questions**

4. In the Scripture passage Mark 5:18–20, we find the healed man requesting to go with Jesus. What is the significance of Jesus telling the man to go home to his family and tell them what the Lord has done?

_____

_____

_____

_____

5. The man who was formerly filled with the devil and so dysfunctional and self-destructive was healed and delivered. He became a man with a powerful testimony and useful for the Kingdom of God. What aspects of this transforming account are most amazing to you?

_____

_____

_____

_____

### Unveiling Life and Purpose

Here was a man who was buried under the garbage of his life and bound by his demons. He was helpless to break free and be healed. His situation seemed hopeless to himself and others. But Jesus came to him with spiritual help that brought healing and freedom. He lifted the man up out of his dysfunction, destruction and despair. He gave him new life and a new purpose. ValueGivers are able to see the person beneath the layers of their dysfunctional behavior. They wade into rescue them, to redeem their lives and their purpose with the help of God.

## Summary Response

⇒ What life lessons have you gleaned from this study session that you will apply as you relate to people who have been deemed "hopeless"?

_____

_____

_____

_____

_____

_____

---

**WORTH CONSIDERATION**

It is unfortunate that some people get written off as beyond hope, throw-away people. Many of us have at times thought that about ourselves. It was certainly true for all of mankind. We were all beyond hope and needed a Savior. We must be grateful that in our own hopeless state Jesus didn't give up on us. The love of God is displayed when we look beyond the person in their desperate condition, sordid dysfunction and failed restorative attempts. What has the appearance as impossible, irreversible and unchangeable is never the case with people. While it is true that some people may not want to change, it is also valid that people need a rescuer when the forces against them are just too powerful to overcome. The power of God is sufficient to overthrow the control of evil. When we care enough to approach the hopeless, we demonstrate that the person has value in spite of wicked stuff. We also introduce the added dimension of help from Heaven. It can make all the difference. Rescuers are difference-makers for the hopeless.

# SESSION 11...*Chapter 9*

# Escape From Smallville

*Read chapter 9 of *The ValueGiver*.

**No man, for any considerable period of time, can wear one face to himself and another to the multitude without finally getting bewildered as to which may be the truth.[6] Nathaniel Hawthorne**

### The Power of the Face Within

Everyone has a "face within." It is our inner self-image. It is the way that we see ourselves. It is the image that we project to the world and the lens through which we view and live our lives. It's the image that describes who we are and how we see ourselves. This image has been shaped by our life experiences, poor choices and the messages we've heard from others. These have carved features into the image that we call our self, which exists in the core of our being. We live our life out of the core orientation of who we believe our self to be. While our perception of our self is very real, it may not be a valid representation of our true self. Our true self is who God created us to be. The distorted self is what we have allowed life and the opinions of others to make us. It is also called the false self, because it's not the true person that God created us to be.

The false self is formed through the image depreciators and diminutive powers that mar and scar the true self. It leaves our face within with such features as failure, inadequate, inferior, shameful, unworthy and unlovable, just to name a few. The good news is that the features of the face of the false self are not terminal and forever etched within our being. Beneath these features, the true self still resides. The person God created us to be and the person that we have the potential to become is beneath the distorted image. God can help us lose the false face and embrace our true face. The power of the face within determines who we are and how we live outwardly. The reality is that we choose who we will be. Regardless of who we've been, we always have the opportunity to become our true self with God's help.

Inferiority is one of the most common features of the false self. It creates the devalued self, the unworthy and inadequate person. The people of the Scripture were people just like each of us. They had issues. Through their struggles of life and faith, we can learn some helpful insights applicable to our lives. The life of Saul portrayed in the Bible is a great example of a man who struggled with inferiority and how it sabotaged his faith, relationships and life goals. He had what we term as the "Spirit of Smallness."

God called Saul to be a leader of God's people. God was aware of Saul's issues, but God's provision of grace and power could enable Saul to emerge into his potential and fulfill his purpose. Saul had the full opportunity to change his face within. God's "front-end" promise to Saul was:

> *The Spirit of the Lord will come upon you in power, and you will prophesy with them; and you will be changed into a different person. Once these signs are fulfilled, do whatever your hand finds to do, for God is with you. I Samuel 10:6–7*

**Scripture Reference:** Read I Samuel 10:20–24

**Discovery Question**

1. This was the ceremony for the crowning of Saul as king of God's people. What a wonderful honor and opportunity! Why was Saul hiding behind the baggage when it was time for him to come forward and step into his destiny?

_____

_____

_____

**Scripture Reference:** Read I Samuel 13:5–13

**Discovery Question**

2. Seeking the Lord before going into battle and receiving blessing was an important practice for the leader and army of God. It was the duty of the priest to make the offering before the Lord. What were the reasons that Saul violated the guidelines of priestly process in giving offerings to the Lord?

_____

_____

_____

**Scripture Reference:** Read I Samuel 15:12

**Discovery Question**

3. Despite Saul's fear and self-reliance, God blessed him and used him to defeat the enemy and bring about a great victory for God's people. Saul's response was to build a monument to himself. In the light of his inadequacy and God's clear provision for the victory, why would Saul build a monument to himself?

_____

_____

_____

**Scripture Reference:** I Samuel 15:13–23

**Discovery Question**

4. Samuel called Saul on his disobedience to the Lord's instructions and identified the spirit of smallness in Saul ("small in your own eyes" I Samuel 15:17). He also brought forward the promise that God had anointed him for the service, meaning Saul had all of the grace and power of God to complete his mission in full obedience to God. Saul stated to Samuel, the priest and prophet, that he did obey the Lord. What is behind his statement that he did obey and fulfill God's instructions?

_____

_____

_____

**Scripture Reference:** I Samuel 15:24

**Discovery Question**

5. Saul finally squares up with the fact that he did not obediently fulfill all of the instructions of the Lord regarding his mission. What is the reason he gives and what does it reveal about Saul?

_____

_____

_____

_____

_____

**Scripture Reference:** I Samuel 18:5–12

**Discovery Question**

6.  What aspects were the root cause of Saul's jealousy toward David?

_____

_____

_____

### Embracing a New Face

It is common for all of us to have some inner "facial features" that are distortions of the true self. It is also true that they illicit behavioral traits that have become habits in our lives to compensate for our inner disorientation. When our inner equilibrium is off, we become unbalanced in some areas of life. At times we underachieve and at other times we overcompensate. We will always live life from the core content of our inner being. We outwardly project our persona to those around us and into the world, through the image lens of the face within.

The good news is that we can get an inner face "makeover." We can trade faces. God offers us the opportunity through relationship with Him and through His grace and power to trade faces: the false self for the true self. As with Saul, through the Spirit of God, we can become a changed person. Regardless of the thick layers of bad experiences, poor choices and image distortions that we've received from others, the true self is deep within us. With God's help, we can become that face and the person God created us to be. We have to be willing to trade in the old and embrace the new. The bottom line of Saul's life was that he could never embrace the new face and his devalued self continued to inject dysfunction into his life.

### Summary Response

⇒  Inferiority is a common affliction in life. There are times everyone has to deal with it in one way or another. But for some people it is an acute condition. It is disabling when it comes to reaching one's destiny. It was that way for Saul. It is also true that we can suffer from various degrees the Spirit of Smallness. It is helpful to identify aspects of inferiority operating in our lives and to take measures to escape from Smallville. It will truly help you to live with less anxiety, with more confidence and to fulfill your destiny. Toward this end, we encourage you to honestly evaluate your life response tendencies in the following Inferiority Inventory. (Please note, if this exercise is being used as part of a small group, it may be most helpful to keep this information private unless individuals choose to share it.)

# Inferiority Inventory

Place a number value between the range of 0-5 with 0 being Never My Tendency and 5 being Very Often My Tendency.

1. ___ I have a tendency to be reluctant to step into opportunities that lead to my destiny.

2. ___ I have a tendency to be susceptible to fear, which tends to lead me to make rather impulsive and rash decisions.

3. ___ I have a tendency to look for ways that I can take credit for things that make me look good.

4. ___ I have a tendency to view and embrace God's directions in light of my ability to fulfill them.

5. ___ I have a tendency of making decisions for my life based mostly on the approval of others.

6. ___ I have the tendency to be suspicious of people, feel threatened by their skills and successes and I view them as competitors.

This brief inventory is to help you identify the presence of inferiority in your life and ways that it may be affecting your life, faith and relationships. These few traits can be indicators of how inferiority may be influencing your life. If your total score was in the range of 0–10, it has little or no affect. If your score was in the range of 10–20, it has some affect. If your score was in the range of 20–30, it has a significant affect. As we have said, most people battle with inferiority issues at some level.

## Commitment to Overcome

Inferiority will prevent us from living life with confidence and fulfilling our purpose and destiny. If you would like to overcome your inferiority issues, God can help. You can begin the process now by changing this inner orientation and the life habits associated with it. The first step is prayer. You ask God to change this area of your life. The following prayer is a means to get you started. You may want to personally add to your prayer in the space provided. Remember, this is just a beginning, but it is a good and necessary step toward overcoming. A more thorough approach, with other steps, may be found in the addendum of *The ValueGiver*. Begin by praying this prayer and then respond further in your own words.

> *God, thank You, for inviting me to bring my issues and burden of inferiority to You. I want to change. I ask that You would help me identify the life experiences and messages that formed the complex*

*of inferiority in my life. As these are revealed to me, I want to give them up to You. I ask that You would take them and change me into a new person. Give me new and appropriate patterns of living; free from the influence of inferiority with its fear, anxiety, suspicion, self-centeredness, control and co-dependency. Change my life and show me more steps to take on the pathway of my healing. I trust Your grace and power to help me in this process. In Jesus' name, amen.*

Continue your prayer or reflection:

_____

_____

_____

_____

_____

_____

_____

_____

_____

_____

_____

_____

---

**WORTH CONSIDERATION**

Most, if not all of us, have struggled with the Spirit of Smallness (inferiority) to one degree or another. It's very common. In our fallen, depreciating world, we settle into a life-level, far below our true created worth. Devaluing life messages and experiences have shaped our inner person, our self image, "the face within." We've self-assessed our value, and often its sum total is severely in the red. We live with an esteem deficit. It affects everything: relationships, career choices, ambitions, future expectations, faith and so on. When we receive God's acceptance, grace and love, He offers us a new image, an image of His original design for us. It's a precious portrait of our treasured worth as His son or daughter. We need to own His portrait for ourselves. We are people of great significance, purpose and destiny.

# SESSION 12...*Chapter 10*

# Calculations, Choices and Changing Channels

*Read chapter 10 of *The ValueGiver.*

**If what we think does not reflect truth, then what we feel does not reflect reality.[7] Neil Anderson**

### Increasing Net Worth

People often calculate their net worth in dollar amounts and in an accounting of tangible assets. But the true worth of a person is their character. The genuine value of a person is found in who they are, not in the things they possess. While we may be living with a depreciated value due to our challenging life experiences, injustices and poor choices, we are invited to take hold of our true created worth. God, our Creator, fashioned us with purpose and initiated our existence in this world. We were neither a happenstance nor an afterthought. We were created with divine intention. It is through our relationship with Him, that we receive our true worth. He loves us, gives us life and considers us significant. He assigned to us a purpose and a destiny. We have the opportunity to make a valuable contribution to the world with our lives.

When we live out of a depreciated value, far beneath God's intention for us, we feel insignificant and unfulfilled; we live aimlessly and without purpose. We have devaluing reference points in our lives, tied to bad past experiences and mistakes we've made. Life messages about us were formed and became ways that we have categorized ourselves. Because of our past, we live with diminished worth. Jesus, The ValueGiver, came to redeem our true worth. He is the *Appreciator.* As difficult as it may for us to believe, through His grace and power, He can restore to us our true net worth.

**Scripture Reference:** Read John 5:1–15

Discovery Questions

1. While the question, *Do you want to get well?* (John 5:6), appears to be a silly question to a man who has been an invalid for thirty-eight years, it was a very good question. Why was Jesus' question a good question?

---

_____

_____

2. The man does not clearly answer the question. What is his reasoning for why he cannot be healed?

_____

_____

_____

_____

## Our Healing Choice

When we are buried under our brokenness, abuse, injustice and life struggles, and our efforts to climb out of our pit of despair have been unsuccessful, we can choose to just settle for a bleak existence. We can even begin to identify with being a hopeless victim of our circumstances. We just become accustomed to our struggles. We hope and believe for nothing beyond the way we've been living. We become so locked in on the afflicted self that we deny the hand of rescue and healing extended to us. Our circumstances may have been the result of unfortunate life events, unfair and unjust abuse from others or our own shameful errors in judgment. While we cannot undo what has been done to us or what we have done, we can make a choice about where life goes from here. Our choice is to remain buried under our stuff, live broken, and identify ourselves as a hopeless victim, or to choose be redeemed with God's help and victoriously overcome our brokenness. The choice is ours. We have to choose to receive God's healing grace for our life afflictions. We have to desire and want to be healed. So Jesus' question to the man was a very good question. It may also be His question to us. _Do you want to get well?_

### Discovery Question

3. What do you see as barriers that make it difficult for people to choose to allow God to bring His healing grace to their life afflictions?

_____

_____

_____

_____

_____

**Scripture Reference:** Read Titus 3:3–8

**Discovery Questions**

4. On the front end of this Scripture passage (Titus 3:3) the apostle Paul is describing our inner- and outer-life conflicts. What issues contribute to the conflicted way of living?

_____

_____

_____

_____

5. The apostle also describes God's provision and antidote for our inner conflict and affliction. Describe in your own words from Titus 3:4–7 the provision of the Lord for us. In other words, what is God's healing antidote for our conflicted condition?

_____

_____

_____

_____

_____

_____

### Facts and Faith

The unfortunate fact of life is that we have all done things and had things done to us that have broken our inner image. It has been scarred and marred through self-afflictions and life afflictions. God created each of us as precious and highly valued, but life in the depreciating world has left us broken. The good news is that we are not broken beyond repair. Through God's kindness and mercy offered to us through the Savior Jesus Christ, we can become a new person. We can ask for His forgiveness and healing. We can have a relationship with God. His Presence, His Spirit, will come and reside in us. He will change our broken image and make us inwardly whole. He will renew and restore our distorted and depreciated image to a true and appreciated one. He will restore our value. We will become valued and valuable. The choice is ours, but we will have to trust Him in faith.

The redemptive plan of God is to restore us to relationship with Himself, grant us our eternal inheritance and to resurrect our intended value, purpose and destiny from the dregs of this depreciating world. Dallas Elder *The ValueGiver p.180*

## Valued and Valuable

God redeems us not only from our sins but also from our depreciating life experiences and the distorted life messages we have derived from them. He embraces us by His grace and love and frees us by His power to live as a precious and purposeful human being created with divine intention. As we realize that we are valued by God, our self-worth appreciates to its true value. We become and live as valued and valuable people. We live and act with a humble but healthy self-respect, dignity and confidence. We fully believe that we have a God-ordained purpose and destiny.

We also begin to view other people differently. Rather than perpetuating the depreciating tendencies of the fallen world, which relentlessly strips people of their respect, dignity, opportunity for advancement, we become redemptive and restorative agents that impart value. Rather than elevating our personal worth by oppressing and deflating others, we rise to new personal heights by appreciating the value of others. The power of being valued releases our potential and frees us to pursue our purpose. This is the power we impart to others. We are redeemed to be redeemers.

## Summary Response

⇒ Describe what you have learned about the importance of being valued as a person. Also describe how our response toward others has the power to appreciate (increase) their self-worth or depreciate (diminish) their self-worth.

_____

_____

_____

_____

_____

_____

_____

_____

_____

_____

---
---
---
---
---
---

**WORTH CONSIDERATION**
The truth is that each of us has been created with divine intention. We were created with sincere affection, supreme worth and careful calculation. The evil of our world can never destroy our true worth unless we allow the truth to be replaced with a lie and continue to mirror the false and distorted image from its untrustworthy sources. We have a choice to make. What self-description will we believe? What image will we embrace for ourselves? We will we be victims or victors. We will we be depreciators or appreciators of people. We will launch forward into our destiny and release others into theirs or live out our remaining days in the valley of broken dreams. The road of life continues from here. You stand at the crossroads of the rest of your life. Choose to trust The ValueGiver. Your best days are ahead of you.

# SESSION 13...*Addendum*

# How to Receive Value and Vision

*Read the Addendum of *The ValueGiver*.

**Everybody has stuff. Our stuff confines us and limits our life. Jesus helps us to sort through our stuff, get through our stuff and get over our stuff. Then, we can freely live out our intended purpose. Dallas Elder *The ValueGiver* p.188**

**Value and Vision**

This section is to help you take the steps to secure your own value, realize your true worth and become the person that God created you to be. Through receiving the assessment of our true value, we receive the vision of our true created image. We can let go of the damaged, distorted and depreciated one and receive our redeemed self. We then can receive the life vision for the pathway toward our purpose.

When we are buried under our "stuff"—poor choices, abuse, rejection, failures and distasteful life experiences—we see only our damaged and devalued self. It distorts and blocks our vision toward our divine destiny. The key to receiving our true value and vision is to get out from under our stuff.

**Summary Response**

⇒ Read and process through the sections, "Securing Your Destiny, Maximizing Your Life Vision" (pages 184–186, *The ValueGiver*) and "Steps To Healing and Freedom" (Pages 186–192, *The ValueGiver*). Be serious and prayerful with a genuine desire to connect with God on the matters that are important to you. Write below your reflection on the issues that were applicable to you as you worked through these sections. Describe the God-experiences, realizations, breakthroughs, healings, affirmations, etc. you received during this exercise.

_____

_____

_____

_____

_____

_____

_____

_____

_____

_____

_____

_____

_____

_____

_____

_____

_____

_____

_____

_____

_____

_____

_____

_____

_____

_____

Determine to live out what you learned and received through this study and your experience connecting with God on the issues relative to your life. Know that you are a valued person in the sight of God and He can redeem you, and you can fully live in your divinely created purpose. He is The ValueGiver and He imparts value. May you become a true representation of The ValueGiver.

# Small Group Leadership Helps

**1. PRAYER** is always a beginning point for any ministry. Small group leaders should ask for God's help in preparation and study time before the group meeting. The leader should always pray in advance for the meeting. Also, once the group membership is established, pray weekly for the people in the group by name. Each meeting should begin and end with prayer. Prayer will limit distractions, allow for more understanding and help the people to be more responsive to the material. People will sense the Presence of God and it will be a good learning environment.

**2. RELATIONAL CHEMISTRY** naturally takes place when people begin to feel comfortable with each other. Remember it takes time for people to begin to interact with one another and to begin to share about personal things. You may need to meet several times for people to become comfortable enough to share openly about their answers to the questions in the study guide. Some questions delve into some very personal areas. Sharing is always voluntary and no one should be put on the spot or forced to share. The group needs to feel like safe place. For this to happen, it must be stressed that what is shared in the group, remains in the group out of respect for the people involved.

**3. LEADERSHIP** is key for the success of the group. The small group leader is the facilitator of the group. The study guide is designed to encourage interaction. The leader should initiate the study and facilitate but not dominate discussion. The leader also needs to be time conscious and help the discussion and interaction of the group to keep moving and not get bogged down. The leader is instrumental in helping each person to feel a part of the group. Some people will talk freely; others are quiet and will need to be coaxed into the interaction. The leader needs to help people feel accepted and affirmed and to not allow more talkative people to dominate the group.

**4. ENRICH** the group experience by being positive, a good listener and showing genuine concern for the things people share. Encourage the people to stay current with their reading and work in the study guide. Healthy accountability within the group motivates people to stay on task and get the most out of the study. The leader's preparation and forethought is primary. Last minute preparation yields a surface group experience. While it is important to follow the study guide in the journey through the material, creative things can be done to add enrichment. For instance, if you have someone who is musically gifted, they could lead a couple of choruses at the beginning. For Session 6, singing the song mentioned, adds to the impact of this session, as the song is beautiful and the words are powerful. You may want to have a meal or fellowship time with snacks and refreshments. Be open to creative inspirations to bring deeper connection with the people involved and the study material. These types of things make the group an enriching, life-changing experience.

# Notes

1. Ray S. Anderson, *The Soul of Ministry* (Louisville, KY: Westminster, Jon Knox Press, 1997), 170.
2. *I Will Change Your Name* by D. J. Butler © 1987 Mercy/Vineyard Publishing (ASCAP). Admin by vineyardmusic.com CCLI # 145139. Used by permission.
3. Yevgeny Yevtushenko as quoted on the Forbes website 1/15/2007.
4. Christine Pohl, *Making Room* (Grand Rapids, Michigan/Cambridge, U.K: William B. Eerdmans Publishing Company, 1999), 16.
5. Gary Smalley, Ministers Conference, Branson, MO, 1999.
6. Nathaniel Hawthorne as quoted by John Eldredge, *Wild at Heart* (Nashville, TN: Thomas Nelson Publishers, 2001), 97.
7. Neil Anderson, *Victory Over The Darkness* (Ventura, CA: Regal Books, 2000), 156.

www.ingramcontent.com/pod-product-compliance
Lightning Source LLC
Chambersburg PA
CBHW081226020426
42331CB00012B/3089